Meyer Lansky: The Infamous Life and Le

By Charles River Editors

About Charles River Editors

Charles River Editors provides superior editing and original writing services across the digital publishing industry, with the expertise to create digital content for publishers across a vast range of subject matter. In addition to providing original digital content for third party publishers, we also republish civilization's greatest literary works, bringing them to new generations of readers via ebooks.

Sign up here to receive updates about free books as we publish them, and visit Our Kindle Author Page to browse today's free promotions and our most recently published Kindle titles.

Introduction

Meyer Lansky

"Don't worry, don't worry. Look at the Astors and the Vanderbilts, all those big society people. They were the worst thieves - and now look at them. It's just a matter of time." – Meyer Lansky

One of America's most infamous mobsters, Meyer Lansky, was also one of the most mysterious, a perplexing, yet inexplicably intriguing individual with multiple reputations. To his admirers, he was in many ways the ultimate genius and survivor within the callous and cut-throat world of 20th century organized crime. Even in adulthood, Meyer was smaller than most, standing anywhere between 4'11" to 5'4", and weighing 136 pounds at his heaviest. He was not merely an intellectual – he was worldly and wise, one who often doled out advice akin to poetry to his children and grandchildren, his gravelly voice oddly soothing. At the same time, he had all the stealth and cunning of a sphinx, and while remarkably even-tempered, gangsters twice his size dared not cross him. To them, he was no more than a wildly ambitious, often misunderstood entrepreneur who trod upon the border between legality and lawlessness with all the mastery of a tightrope artist. He was, above all, the definition of humility, one whose "handshake was worth more than any contract," and a man who actively dodged the spotlight that doggedly tailed him until the end of his days.

Conversely, most will quickly concede that while Lansky was an exceptionally clever criminal, he was a criminal all the same, and the crimes of this dark horse were unforgivable. Meyer was a fraudulent, tax-evading crook whose massive fortune was literally made off the bodies of countless victims. He was a silver-tongued fiend who preyed on the weak and impressionable, plying them with booze and drugs and feeding their gambling addictions.

Lansky, whose most famous nickname remains the "Mob's Accountant," was one of the few gangsters of his era to die in old age, and he was never pinched for anything more serious than gambling. It's believed he made upwards of $20 million in his time as a mobster, but some still claim he was never the mogul the media painted him out to be. Instead, they assert that he was an expendable middleman, and that he was an overzealous rogue who squandered away whatever fortune he had.

Meyer Lansky: The Infamous Life and Legacy of the Mob's Accountant profiles the controversial life of one of organized crime's most notorious figures. Along with pictures of important people, places, and events, you will learn about Meyer Lansky like never before.

Becoming Meyer Lansky

"I don't know how fully convinced you are of the importance of learning, but in due time, you will realize the importance of school." – attributed to Meyer Lansky by his grandson

Maier Suchowljansky was born in the dicey city of Grodno, Russia (now Belarus) in 1902. His parents, Max and Yetta Suchowljansky, christened him after the celebrated 2nd century Jewish Rabbi Meir, who imparted to various sages the gift of enlightenment. The pair were comparable in various ways, including that they were both highly intelligent, persecuted, and forced to struggle in a tempestuous environment they had no control over. But it was there that their paths diverged.

Obscurity seemed to be a major element of Maier's life from the very beginning. His earliest childhood records, such as his enrollment applications for one of his schools, list his birthday as the August 28, but his date of birth on his immigration documents was registered as July 4. As the story goes, his grandparents, Benjamin and Basha, knew only their grandson's birth year, leaving it up to the immigration officers to assign one to him. One could say this episode was the initiation of the alienation he would feel for the rest of his life. In the same breath, one could say it heralded the emergence of his lesser-known patriotism.

For the first eight years of his life, Maier and his family did their best to persevere in the oppressive, violently anti-Semitic climate of early 20th century Russia. Russian and Polish Jews retaliated in kind, forming numerous institutions that attempted to defend Jewish neighborhoods against anti-Semitic mobs. Their efforts were noble, but with the cards stacked against them, they could only do so much. A scrupulous, but low-earning garment presser, Max Suchowljansky struggled to maintain the roof over the family of four, and for years, he scraped by the best he could, wishfully pining for a brighter day.

Much to his dismay, the anti-Jewish sentiment at home was rapidly degenerating. The dawn of the 1900s saw a dramatic upswing in lootings, rape, and senseless murders that targeted Jewish populations across the empire. A passage from the diary of journalist and Bolshevik revolutionary Isaac Babel described one such pogrom, noting that the assailants "cut off beards...assembled 45 Jews in the marketplace, led them to the slaughteryard, tortures, cut out tongues, wails heard all over the square..." One of the worst ordeals suffered by Jews transpired in 1903 in Kishinev, roughly 650 miles south of Grodno. On Easter Sunday, throngs of anti-Semites plundered 1,500 Jewish storefronts and countless homes and set them ablaze, savagely laying waste to two-thirds of the city in just two days. More heartbreaking yet, 49 Jewish residents were slain, 92 were severely injured, and numerous others were raped. The Suchowljanskys themselves fell victim to an unrelated attack when a relative's arm was hacked off while he was attempting to defend himself.

In 1909, Max hopped aboard a boat destined for Ellis Island, determined to seek out a more promising future for his growing family. He embarked on this journey alone, and he shortened his surname to "Lansky" upon his arrival. Only after securing himself a job and a dingy apartment in Brooklyn two years later did the rest of the family follow him to New York.

The Suchowljansky boys, 8-year-old Maier and his younger brother Jacob, clung onto the railing of the rickety boat, their gleaming eyes widening at the sight of the Statue of Liberty. All the stories young Maier had heard about this fantastical place swirled in his head all at once; this was where one could pursue their dreams with no restraints, a land of opportunities and second chances. As an adult, Lansky would later recall his 8-year-old self's idealistic expectations of the United States, "a place of angels...somewhat like heaven."

Unfortunately, the family's living situation was far more inconstant than Max had hoped. Maier spent much of his early years in America bouncing around from one squalid apartment to another. They resided in the crowded complex on 240 Ocean Parkway, Brooklyn until 1912, and then lived on 33 Chester Street for a few months before relocating to 894 Rockaway Avenue, where they temporarily settled for the following two years. Finally, sometime in early 1914, Max made the pivotal decision to move his family to the Lower East Side of Manhattan, into an impoverished, but vibrant Jewish ghetto. There, the Suchowljansky family resided in a compact 3rd floor apartment on 546 Grand Street.

Initially, Maier and his siblings attended PS 84 (now Jose de Diego) in Brooklyn, where his name was first Americanized to "Meyer," before transferring to PS 34 on Sheriff and Broome. During this time, Max continued to toil away at the textile factory on average between 54-63 hours a week in abysmally dangerous conditions for practically no pay. According to his biographers, young Meyer secretly resented his father's inadequacy when it came to providing for the family, as well as his ignorance towards solid investments and the concept of savings.

Meyer was, for the most part, a collected and rather pragmatic child. The bright boy got above-average grades in school and was quite sociable, but he clearly preferred to keep to himself, with his nose buried in books. As much as he enjoyed reading books of all genres, it was with numbers that he truly excelled.

Given the time and environment, Meyer was not much different from other Jewish boys his age. He was disciplined, played well with his siblings and peers, and did what was expected of him, including chores, *cheder* (Hebrew school for Jewish children), serving *cholent* (a slow-cooked, savory Jewish stew) every Saturday, and so forth. He dodged, and rarely, if ever instigated a fight at school or on the streets. Of course, this isn't to say that he was never in one, and while it wasn't his style to start a scuffle, he wasn't opposed to finishing one.

One afternoon, as a 12-year-old Meyer made his way home with a tinfoil-wrapped platter of food in his hands, he found himself waylaid by a band of teenage Irish hoodlums. Their ringleader, brandishing a switchblade, taunted Meyer for his size and hurled numerous anti-Semitic epithets at him. At first, Meyer attempted to sidestep his way out of the situation, but when the ringleader lunged forth, demanding that he yank down his pants to check if he was circumcised, Meyer sprung into action. He flung the plate on the ground, picked up the largest and most jagged fragment of the shattered dish, and slashed his tormentor across the throat. The rest of Meyer's assailants pounced on him like rabid football players, whaling on the kid until a passing group of adults pulled them off one another.

15-year-old Meyer had just completed the 8th grade when he had to cease his education and enter the workforce. He was smaller than most other teenagers, and though he much preferred to sit down with a good book, the dexterous young man proved to be a fine machinist. He was first employed at a local tool-and-die shop called the "D & L Tool Company," which once stood on Center Street, part of an assembly line of sorts that manufactured dies, fixtures, molds, and an array of other tools. He later assisted in the manufacturing of wooden printing presses at the R & Hoe Company, just a few blocks away from home, before scoring a post at Richard Mirror Works somewhere along Greene Street.

It was only in 1921 that the industrious young man, now employed as an auto mechanic, began to dip his toe into murkier waters. Like the rest of his colleagues, young Meyer punctually serviced the vehicles on the agenda assigned to him, which earned him the trust of his superiors, so much so that they were either blissfully or consciously ignorant of the plateless cars that suspicious customers regularly brought to him for remodeling after hours. The siren call of the streets, a volatile, but lucrative place of business, became far too difficult for the hungry, but financially floundering young man to resist.

As a result, it was on the streets that Meyer's penchant for logic and numbers continued to blossom. He found himself especially productive while observing the craps games conducted on corners and in alleys. It was also during one particular game of craps that he was dealt one of his first major life lessons. Before Shabbat one afternoon, Meyer's mother handed him a nickel and instructed him to settle the family's tab with the baker around the corner. On his way to the bakery, however, he chanced upon an ongoing game of craps. Believing that he had sufficiently studied the game from afar, he decided to partake in the next game, hoping to double or perhaps even triple the nickel he was prepared to wager. Unfortunately, however, Meyer lost the nickel on his first roll.

With a heavy head and his tail tucked between his legs, Meyer confessed to his mother what he had done, and he was forced to spend the entire service that morning soaking in shame. Never again would he gamble, especially when the money was not his, for the odds would most likely never be in his favor. From now on, Meyer vowed, he would govern the game. As an adult, he would remark, "There's no such thing as a lucky gambler; there are just the winners and losers.

The winners are those who control the game...all the rest are suckers. The only man who wins is the boss."

It was also on the rough and tumble streets of New York City that Meyer first became acquainted with an individual who would become his lifelong comrade and "business" partner. Legend has it that he was on his way home from school one afternoon when he decided to hover over a craps game for a bit. All was going swell until a younger participant, no older than 11, kicked the dice aside and accused his opponent of cheating. A tussle soon erupted, which resulted in one of the older boys shoving the 11-year-old to the ground. Meyer initially froze when he saw the glimmer of what appeared to be a loaded pistol fall out of the boy's pocket. Acting quickly, the boy's opponent scooped up the pistol and aimed it at the 11-year-old. Fortunately for the younger boy, as soon as Meyer heard the unmistakable cock of the gun, he leapt in front of the child and wrestled the pistol out of his opponent's hands. Before anyone else could react, the shriek of police whistles pierced the air, prompting the boys to scatter at once.

The 11-year-old seized Meyer by the elbow and led him down an alleyway congested with pushcarts, sprinting into the distance as fast as their legs would carry them. Once the breathless boys were safe, the 11-year-old, who would identify himself as Benjamin Siegel, thanked Meyer for saving his life and offered him a precious bit of advice as a token of his gratitude. "Never let [the cops] see you with a gun in your hand," the boy rasped. "Never let [them] see who you are." Benjamin, who earned himself the nickname "Bugsy" from his fellow hoodlums on account of his alleged manic spells and "propensity for sudden cold-blooded violence," was the antithesis of the analytical and cool-headed Meyer, but the pair nevertheless formed a tight bond that few could rationalize.

Bugsy Siegel

It was about a year or two later that Meyer forged another lifelong bond, one even unlikelier than the last. At the time, it was challenging, to say the least, for folks from any background to take a stroll down the streets of the Lower East Side without being hassled by one of the Irish, Italian, or Jewish gangs constantly roaming around the neighborhood, and Jews walking home or manning their pushcarts by their lonesome were the gangs' favorite targets for shakedowns. Young Meyer was designated a target during his route home from work, and on one occasion, he ducked into an alleyway just as he did every day, during which he came across a loitering band of teenage Italian gangsters. The hooligans quickly detected the mousy, dark-haired boy on their radar, and with mischievous smirks on their faces, they homed in on him. Meyer halted in his tracks, glancing at the bats, clubs, and the assortment of blunt and sharp objects they wielded menacingly in their hands as they demanded that he cough up – ironically – "protection money." If Meyer forked over the 10 cents a week from his wages, as he was told, they would make certain that he remain untouchable to all other gangs, most importantly theirs.

Shakedown victims who were vastly outnumbered typically gave up the dime, no questions asked. Meyer, on the other hand, scorned the illogical concept of settling a bill he did not owe, particularly for unneeded services. As such, he articulated this to the pockmarked ringleader with a distinctive lazy eye, a boy named Charles Luciano, and coolly attempted to walk around him. The rest of the gang stepped forward, snarling as they raised their weapons in the air. As Luciano reined them in, he ordered the fearless youngster to stay put, and, to the incredulity of his flunkies, extended a hand to the Jewish Meyer.

Lucky Luciano

If street ruffians and mobsters were puzzled by the relationship between Meyer and Bugsy, they were utterly mystified by the connection between Meyer and Lucky Luciano. To start with, Lucky, who got his name when he survived a throat slashing a few years later, was an enterprising and calculating young man, but like Bugsy, his capacity for violence was alarming. Between the years of 1916 and 1936, he was apprehended a total of 25 times on charges of assault, extortion, theft, robbery, blackmail, and unlicensed gambling, yet he would serve almost no time in prison.

Furthermore, the pair found a way to rise above the long-established race-related demarcations among the territorial gangs, reaching an elevation that allowed them to see past their differences and focus only on their shared interests. Bugsy reportedly said that Lansky and Luciano "were more than brothers, they were like lovers. They would just look at each other, and you would know that a few minutes later one of them would say what the other was thinking."

What Lucky, Bugsy, and Meyer's future associates found most admirable about the pint-sized, but plucky youngster were his integrity and his comfort in his own identity. Another anecdote that highlighted his honor occurred during a basketball game against a team of Irish teenagers. The Irish boys had taken a liking to Meyer, but fearing backlash from their own kind, they requested to call him "Mike" instead to conceal his Jewish roots. To this, Meyer staunchly refused, and he opted to bow out of all future games.

By 1918, a 16-year-old Meyer and 12-year-old Bugsy had set a somewhat stable foundation for what would one day become the Bugs and Meyer Mob. According to Lansky, "I told [Bugsy, the youngest member of the gang], that he could be my number two. He was young, but very brave. His big problem was that he was always ready to rush in first and shoot – to act without thinking." Impulsiveness aside, Bugsy was dauntless (at times to a fault), eager to please, and often had the ability to think outside of the box, making for a perfect partner as the fast-thinking and fast-acting brawn to Meyer's brain.

Since the insightful duo had longevity over profits in mind, they started small, orchestrating and managing their own "floating craps games." Meyer, who was never the type to be hostile without provocation, felt it wiser to build a business around indomitable vices, especially the locals' addictions to gambling. Even so, it was supposedly his policy to conduct all his games honestly so as to retain a roster of repeat customers and preserve his reputation, naturally expanding his customer base.

At the same time, with the supplementary cash he was now raking in, the glint of ambition in his eye grew steadily brighter. It made less and less sense to invest hundreds of back-breaking hours into his factory jobs and being rewarded only a measly $45 (roughly $587 today) each month.

In late 1921, the crew, which now included Meyer's brother Jacob, Samuel "Red" Levine, Meyer "Mike" Wassell, Joseph "Doc" Stacher, Irving "Tabbo" Sandler, and a few others, began to branch out to various new ventures. For starters, Meyer was no longer simply camouflaging cars for bootleggers; exploiting the resources he was provided at the auto shop, he began to re-skin vehicles jacked by his colleagues before the mob pawned them off themselves.

The Jewish thugs, seemingly taking a page from Lucky's playbook, also began to extort small business owners for protection money, predominantly against rival Irish and Italian circles. Other petty crimes the mob concerned themselves with included loan sharking, small stock manipulations, roughing up Italian and Irish toughs who harassed their Jewish charges, and burglary, including reportedly fleeing from a bank with more than $8,000 (approximately $98,000 today) on one occasion. For a time, Meyer also moonlighted as a "back room" agent and lookout at an underground gambling joint. He was so productive in his endeavors that he was even employed by a local union to sort out a labor dispute via the mob's "disciplinary" methods.

In hindsight, all of the above would seem like child's play considering what lay in store for the spirited, albeit somewhat misguided young man.

Meyer the Entrepreneur

"All you have to do is recognize an opportunity." – attributed to Meyer Lansky

The quick learner that he was, Lansky absorbed and eliminated the inefficiencies that plagued his operations in his earlier days. As such, the growth his "businesses" experienced was meteoric. Lansky eventually resigned from his post as a mechanic to establish his own car and truck rental garage, which allegedly doubled as a warehouse for "hot" vehicles and other contraband.

Soon, the Bugs and Meyer Mob crossed paths with and forged another strategic "business" relationship with a notorious ring of thugs known as the "Broadway Mob." Chaired by Joe Adonis and managed by Lucky Luciano and Frank Costello, the Broadway Mob oversaw one of the largest bootlegging networks during the Prohibition Era. It was apparently Arnold Rothstein, the chief patron of the Broadway Mob's operations, who employed the Bugs and Meyer Mob to guard the Broadway Mob's illicit alcohol shipments. The new hires, who eventually merged their contacts and operations with that of the Broadway Mob, were also tasked with heisting cash from banks and hijacking furs and other valuable goods to assist in the financing of liquor batches.

Costello

Prohibition, which began on January 16, 1920, was poorly planned and appallingly executed in more ways than one. For one, the ban on the manufacture and sale of booze did almost nothing to curb the nation's drinking habits. Moreover, it presented to the underworld a new, grossly profitable market on a silver platter, and it allowed for the birth of a slew of ingenious tactics and the discovery of loopholes, leading to a major upswing in the world of organized crime.

A study that investigated more than 30 large cities in the United States between 1920 and 1921 found that crime rates spiked by 24%, and drug addiction rose by a staggering 44.6%. On top of the 11.4% increase in police department expenses, Prohibition spawned a new wave of territorial wars among the various bootlegging operations around the country. Hershel Kessler, a retired gangster from Detroit, later interpreted and vindicated the mentality of the Prohibition-era bootleggers in an interview with historian Robert Rockaway in 1989: "People wanted booze, they wanted dope, they wanted to gamble, and they wanted broads. For a prince, we provided them with these amusements. We only gave them what they wanted."

Many credit Arnold Rothstein with catapulting Lansky to the next stage of his storied, clandestine career. The normally collected Lansky, who first met Rothstein at a bar mitzvah, was apparently star-struck and could only mumble a few words in response to his idol during the entirety of their six-hour conversation. Rothstein, described by historian Leo Katcher as "the J. P. Morgan of the underworld," was to Lansky a self-made entrepreneur who cashed in his first million by the age of 30. He first shot to fame as a gambling and managing tycoon in the underbelly of New York society through his numbers rackets, gambling joints, and racetracks, and he gained further notoriety through his alleged involvement in the fixing of the 1919 World

Series. Lansky himself would later heap more praise on Rothstein: "[He] had the most remarkable brain. He understood business instinctively, and I'm sure that if he had been a legitimate financier, he would have been just as rich as he became with his gambling and the other rackets he ran." Even Lucky, who fancied himself ungovernable, "worshiped" Rothstein. Luciano recalled, "He taught me how to dress…how to use knives and forks and thinks like that at the dinner table, about holding a door open for a girl. If [Rothstein] had lived a little longer, he could've made me pretty elegant."

For his part, Rothstein considered Lansky a kindred spirit. Taking the 20-something young man under his wing, Rothstein sharpened his protégé's skills and foresight, and he spelled out what it took to expand his operations. Most importantly, Rothstein urged Lansky to regard his schemes, first and foremost, as a business.

Apart from the illegal spirits they imported from Scotland and peddled to their unquenchable customers, the collaborating mobs – with Lansky employed as their "numbers guy" – are also believed to have sunk their teeth into prostitution, as well as the distribution of heroin and other narcotics, a sector with a loyal customer base that extended all the way to Europe.

Lansky, among others, would later claim that it was not just lowlifes, but some of the most "important people in the country" who milked the cash cow gifted to them by Prohibition, and chroniclers point to the following incident as proof behind said claim. One stormy evening in 1927, a convoy transporting Irish whiskey in the southern neck of New England was suddenly ambushed by the henchman of a rival bootlegger who didn't take kindly to trespassing in the area under his jurisdiction. The commissioner of the ambushed convoy, reportedly none other than U.S. Ambassador to the United Kingdom Joseph P. Kennedy, Sr., was beleaguered by the debilitating loss, which resulted in the deaths of 11 of his employees. He was then made to shell out "a fortune" in damages and losses, as well as reparations to the family members of his deceased men. Lansky was especially knowledgeable about this particular episode, because it was he who had allegedly hatched the plans for the ambush.

In the autumn of 1928, roughly a year after Kennedy's convoy was assailed, Rothstein lumbered out of an elevator and crumpled to the floor in a heap, clutching the gaping gunshot wound in his gut. Mortally wounded in a hotel suite, he was later rushed to a Manhattan hospital, where he was pronounced dead shortly thereafter. The hit is believed to have been carried out by Dutch Schultz in retaliation for the murder of his friend at the hands of a Rothstein associate.

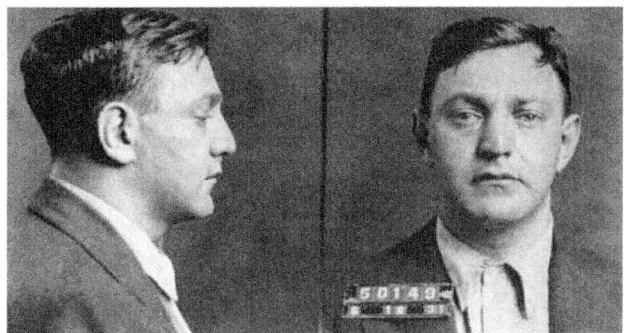

Dutch Schultz

Lansky anticipated his mentor's demise, but he was still crushed by the news. Be that as it may, Rothstein's permanent retirement was in many ways a blessing in disguise, for Lansky and Luciano jointly inherited the operations left behind by their most trusted adviser. By the end of the 1920s, the Broadway Mob and Bugs and Meyer Mob had become the principal suppliers of imported whiskey to some of the most frequented underground speakeasies, such as the *Silver Slipper*, the *Stork Club, Jack White's,* and the *21 Club*. They were pricier than most other bootleggers, but the quality of their shipments never disappointed. Even the liquor stored in their reserve – inferior booze purchased from mobster Waxey Gordon in Philadelphia – was regarded by the masses as incomparably superior to the watered-down booze hawked by other local gangsters.

To strengthen their grip on the bootlegging enterprise, Lansky and Lucky acquired interests in dozens of popular nightclubs and speakeasies, and eventually numerous other lands, homes, and properties in Manhattan. The NYPD officers who scrambled to infiltrate the mobs' operations, often fruitlessly, branded them a sadistic and "vicious" network. One detective assigned to the impulsive Bugsy painted him as a hands-on type of criminal who "got his kicks out of seeing his victims suffering, groaning, and dying." Fortunately for Bugsy, Lansky and Lucky were sweeping up the breadcrumbs he recklessly left behind from the very beginning, purchasing the silence of all those who could be bought. Luciano claimed, "Within a year, we was buyin' influence all over Manhattan, from lower Broadway all the way up to Harlem."

In *The Testament of Lucky Luciano*, a self-penned memoir, Lucky credited the astute and intuitive Lansky with leading them to the next phase of their swelling enterprise, as well as solidifying the "corporate structure" their organizations were modeled after. The uneducated Lucky also commended Lansky for the patience he exhibited towards him. In one of his most memorable moments with the soft-spoken Lansky, Lucky recounted that Lansky, who was five years his junior, recited passages from a book entitled "*Making Profits*" by William Taussig. He told Lucky, "This writer talks about a thing called the law of supply and demand. What he says applies to us right now. If you have a lot of what people want and can't get, then you can supply the demand and shovel in the dough. In other words, that's what we ought to do with whiskey – get plenty of it, good, uncut stuff right off the boat, and then sell it a high price to...people who don't have brains enough not to drink it." This concept, which would become one of organized crime's primary creeds, was coined "Lansky's Law."

Of course, Luciano wasn't the only one giving Lansky the credit. As former mafioso Joseph Bonanno of the Bonanno Crime Family put it, "[Lansky] was the financial whiz behind Lucky Luciano's success."

This unorthodox union was also mutually beneficial for both when they sought to break the control of the so-called Mustache Petes, an early generation Italian-American mafia that stressed the importance of adhering to old-school traditions and "sticking with one's own kind." Instead, they discovered the promise in the diversity of resources and the potential profits they could achieve by pooling together their capital, supplies, and experience in various fields.

This was another page they took from Rothstein's playbook. Rothstein was among the first to breach the antiquated rules by engaging in business and partnerships with Sicilians, Italians, Irish, and Jewish thugs alike. Moreover, Rothstein personally avoided partaking in booze, narcotics, or even tobacco. As such, the up-and-comers were taught never to cave into the temptations of their own supply, and to regard it as strictly inventory.

Murder, Inc.

"We only kill each other." – attributed to Bugsy Siegel

Rothstein's coveted operations were divvied up amongst Lansky, Lucky, Bugsy, Frank Erickson, and a few other associates shortly after his demise, and though concrete evidence remains scarce, authorities believe it was around this time that Rothstein's successors simultaneously launched a nefarious new wing known as "Murder, Inc," also known as "The Combination," or "The Syndicate." The Syndicate, named as such to underscore the dubious patchwork of "talents" possessed by its members, was apparently immensely well-connected and more than simply solvent, allowing them to bribe senators, judges, sheriffs, detectives, and other politicians and law enforcement so as to scrub away their tracks. The Syndicate's portfolio was manifold – they, too, purveyed booze, women, a rainbow of narcotics, cards tables, and chips at their secret speakeasies and casinos, but they were also involved in labor and commercial racketeering, burglaries, bank hold-ups, vehicular hijackings, and so on. The organization's most disconcerting undertaking, however, was its department of assassins; the Syndicate's contract killers were eerily prolific, too, and are said to have been responsible for over 1,000 deaths across the country.

In May 1929, Bugsy took the opportunity to organize a conference between a number of underworld figures that he had become acquainted with over the last 10 years, though to anyone who asked, he was celebrating his honeymoon with Esta in Atlantic City. The meeting was hosted by Enoch "Nucky" Johnson, the political boss and crooked sheriff of Atlantic County, New Jersey, and was attended by Lansky, Al Capone, Moses Annenberg, Dutch Schultz, and other notable players from New Jersey, Boston, Chicago, Philadelphia, Kansas, Detroit, Florida, Ohio, and New Orleans.

Noticeably absent on the list were Giuseppe "Joe the Boss" Masseria and Salvatore Maranzano. These Italian crime lords, along with a number of other Irish mob bosses, were regarded as impulsive and needlessly violent. Their vengeful antics and thriving, but delicate operations were as messy as they were indiscreet. Thus, as powerful and well-connected as they were, they were deemed detrimental to the brand. It was time, argued those present, for them to cut the dead weight.

Masseria

The attendees also brainstormed remedies to the current problems at hand, such as the inevitable end to Prohibition. In order to survive, they had to consider legitimizing their bootlegging operations into legal liquor manufacturing companies and storefronts. Moreover, they had to merge together their gambling and sporting sectors, while also expanding their operations nationwide to locate new sources of revenue.

The Syndicate's board of directors was composed of Italians, Jews, and one or two Irish mobsters. Lansky, Lucky, Bugsy, Louis Lepke, and Dutch Schultz are all believed to have completed stints as chairpersons of The Combination for some time. Lansky was allegedly among the men who designed the process all of the Syndicate's hitmen were made to adhere to.

To begin with, one had to first submit a request for the murder in question, which was then reviewed and voted on by the chairpersons. These conferences, described as miniature "court hearings," were normally conducted in hotel rooms and the rears of restaurants after hours. *Billy Gwon's Chinese Restaurant, Dinty Moore's,* and the *Savoy Plaza Hotel Barber Shop* are said to have been some of the places that Lansky himself not only frequented, it was also where he held many of these meetings. Following a green light from the board, the contract was assessed and appraised by Lansky; no contract was executed, they say, until it received Lansky's personal stamp of approval. As per the Syndicate's policy, under no circumstances should an assassination motivated by a personal grudge be authorized. Most who were placed behind the cross-hairs were those who violated the brotherhood's bylaws, or presented themselves as hurdles in the progress of their enterprise. Last, but not least, members were prohibited from targeting politicians, government workers, journalists, or civilians so as to keep the probing eyes to a minimum.

The seven-step manual that dictated the contract killers' standard operating procedures was also allegedly devised by Lansky. Following the approval of the contract, an out-of-state agent was selected and presented with the proposal. Once the contract was assigned to the assassin, he stocked up on weapons and packed a small bag with roughly a week's worth of clothes and supplies. Next, the assassin commuted to the neighborhood of his mark, and tracked down his place of residence. He then stationed himself at a blind spot and observed his mark for a few days to memorize the target's schedule as well as to flesh out other details of the impending assassination, such as identifying a secluded location for the main event.

Pistols, ice picks, and bare hands were the most commonly utilized weapons. As soon as the job was completed, the corpses were dismembered and tossed into the river, body parts tethered to weights, or burnt beyond identification in faraway fields or pits. Finally, the assassin hopped aboard a train and booked it, making certain to "take care of" any unfortunate witnesses.

As predicted by those at the conference, Masseria and Maranzano, who belonged to an older class of gangsters derogatorily referred to by up-and-coming mobsters as "Mustache Petes," declared war on one another the following year, now remembered as the "Castellammarese War." When that touched off, the organizers of the meeting convened again at a smaller gathering, and though there was mild remorse expressed by some who previously worked with both of the older men, the consensus was that the time had come to snuff out the wildcards.

As much as loyalty and brotherhood are glorified in the movies, most gangsters in the real world are motivated by profits and have no qualms turning on their allies in the name of business. In the same breath, it was not unlikely for rivals to overlook their differences and work together to achieve a common goal, should the situation call for it.

Indeed, that helps explain tempestuous relationship between Bugsy, Lansky, Lucky, and Masseria. Back in the mid-1920s, when the younger three continued carving out a name for themselves in the illegal gambling scene of New York, they snapped up a large chain of bookmaking operations and forged solid relationships with both politicians and police in the Lower East Side through hefty bribes and substantial favors. Infuriated by the unlicensed business on their turf, Masseria and Arnold Rothstein, the latter a former ally of the Bugs and Meyer Mob, set out to teach the intruders a lesson. One evening, a burly band of thugs employed by Masseria and Rothstein descended upon the trio's hangout and proceeded to assail Bugsy, Lansky, and the customers of the craps game in operation at the time. As the injured parties lay writhing on the ground, the thugs hovered over Bugsy and Lansky and informed them that this was merely a warning. The newcomers were told to either clear out or pay their employers a percentage of their profits, plus interest, to make up for their indiscretions. Disobey them again, they warned, and there would be no next time.

However, rather than yield to Masseria and Rothstein's demands, the trio regrouped and responded with an ambush of their own. The scrimmage escalated to such a point that the cops were notified, which ultimately led to the arrest of Lansky, Bugsy, and a few other accomplices. Much to the chagrin of Masseria and Rothstein, despite the clear proof of Bugsy and Lansky's violent tendencies, the two were so influential that they were let off with a measly $2 fine.

When the Castellammarese War began to tilt in the favor of Masseria's rival, the trio was more than happy to reach out to Maranzano and strike up a deal. The terms of the negotiation were fairly straightforward - if Maranzano agreed to swallow his pride and back down, thereby ending a frivolous dispute that would only certainly spell trouble for all of them, they would take out Masseria. It took some convincing, but Maranzano finally agreed.

On the 15th of April, 1931, 4 hitmen, believed to be Bugsy, Vito Genovese, Joe Adonis, and Albert "Mad Hatter" Anastasia, snuck in through the back door of Nuova Villa Tammaro, a popular seafood joint in Coney Island. Masseria had been playing cards with his evening companion, none other than the smooth-spoken Lucky Luciano himself, who had conveniently excused himself to the bathroom just before the four men burst into the room and unleashed 20 bullets on Masseria. Four pierced the oblivious Masseria in the back and one struck him in the head, killing him instantly. Masseria's killers were never arrested.

With Masseria out of the picture, Maranzano wasted no time seizing the reins and reorganizing the consequently chaotic Italian-American mob scene in New York. Five all-Italian families were formed, and Maranzano installed himself at the top of the totem pole by declaring himself the *"capo di tutt'i capi,"* or the "Boss of All Bosses."

In the early 1930s, during the crescendo of the Castellammarese War, Lansky's contract killer management services were supposedly requested by none other than his partner, Lucky. At this stage, the power-starved Lucky, who longed to commandeer the Italian-American mafias, was desperate to snuff out the lone figure he believed obstructed his path to the pinnacle: Salvatore Maranzano.

Matters swiftly soured in just a matter of months. When Maranzano wised up to the hit out against him, he hastened to act first, and employed one Vincent "Mad Dog" Coll to defuse and dismantle the ticking time bomb that was Lucky, as well as his close comrade, Vito Genovese. As the story goes, when Lansky was tipped off about Lucky's soon-to-be murder, he warned his friend at once and aided him in escaping the ambush. It was then that Lansky, who was initially reluctant about executing such a prominent figure, agreed to stiff the growing predicament.

On September 10, 1931, a quartet of mobsters hired by Lansky, posing as IRS agents, entered the Helmsley Building and proceeded to the 9th floor, where Maranzano's main headquarters was situated. As soon as the elevator doors parted, the assailants disarmed Maranzano's security team before storming into the mark's office. The startled Maranzano was flung against the wall and his chest, stomach, and face punctured by a blade four times before one of them seized him by the neck, cutting off his airway with his fingers. Then, they fired six bullets into the convulsing and bloodied Maranzano before slinking off and leaving him for dead. The Jewish out-of-towners were specially selected to throw the investigators off Lucky's scent.

This was not the end of the bloodbath. In just two days, 40-50 associates tied to Maranzano, as well as suspected witnesses and loose-lipped conspirators, were butchered. Among the dead were Sam Monaco, James Marino, and Louis Rosso, all of whom were grievously tortured, murdered, quartered, and laid to rest on the riverbed. Many say it was Lansky who choreographed these follow-up assassinations, effectively slaughtering dozens without ever pulling the trigger himself.

With the last of the Mustache Petes gone, Lucky planted himself upon the vacant throne at the head of the Five Families. That said, he retired the title of *"capo di tutt'i capi"* and split the power amongst five bosses, much like the Buffalo and Chicago chapters, in a bid to stave off any future wars and unnecessary bloodshed. All five positions were assigned to other Italian mobsters, but Bugsy and Lansky were regarded as "valued associates" all the same, and they were permitted to conduct business on what was now Lucky's turf as they pleased.

It was only after the death of Masseria and Maranzano that the outside world really took notice, and the group became an invaluable tool of powerful mob bosses along the East Coast, for it was more than just an outfit of dexterous contract killers, they were methodical and cautious, careful not to leave any tracks. Above all, in the rare times that they slipped up and found themselves detained by authorities, they remained tight-lipped "professionals" (for the most part), and either bribed their way out of the pickle, or served their time with their head down without implicating their employers.

Altogether, Murder, Inc. is estimated to have slain 400-1,000, with Bugsy himself supposedly responsible for the deaths of anywhere between 10-30 people. This arm of the group, which operated out of Midnight Rose, a 24-hour candy shop and cafe located on the corner of Saratoga and Livonia Avenue in Brownsville, Brooklyn, originally handled contracts along the East Coast, but their missions eventually took them across the continent, at times butchering their victims in Detroit and even Florida. The brick storefront, with the words "CANDY," "SODA," and "CIGAR," printed across the canopy awning and display windows brimming with boxes of toffees, chocolates, peppermint swirls, fruity lollipops, and other sugary confectionery, looked like nothing more than a whimsical little shop. Mrs. Rosie Gold, the sweet little 60-year-old immigrant who owned Midnight Rose, seemed even more unassuming. It was precisely her infectious smile and warm hospitality that made her a priceless asset to the executioners. In reality, Rosie was involved in loansharking, fraud, bail bonds, and a slew of other rackets with her son, Sam "The Dapper" Siegal, and her daughter, Shirley Herman. And while Rose was classified as illiterate, she was evidently a calculating and far-sighted businesswoman. When authorities eventually dug into her past, they were startled at the number of shady dealings she was implicated in, including a bank statement revealing that over $400,000 (roughly $5,864,000 today) had been deposited and withdrawn from her personal account in less than 12 months.

While there were plenty who struggled to make a good, honest living despite the unimaginable hardships brought by the devastating 1929 crash of the New York Stock Exchange, it is easy to see why so many opted for the glitter, fast money, and fame the prosperous world of organized crime had to offer. For starters, every member of Murder, Inc was paid a sizable base salary, and another bonus ranging anywhere between $1,000 ($14,660 today) and $5,000 ($73,300) per kill. Moreover, each member's families were granted numerous privileges, including a guaranteed pension if the hitman died in the "line of duty." Those who were nabbed by law enforcement were also promised a formidable army of defense attorneys.

Two separate divisions made up the body of Murder, Inc., divided between the Jews and the Italians. Hitmen were typically commissioned to wipe out marks belonging to their ethnicity. Bugsy, and later Louis "Lepke" Buchalter (the only American mob boss in history to get the chair), oversaw the division of Jewish hitmen, while Albert "the Mad Hatter" Anastasia presided over their Italian counterparts.

Anastasia

Al Aumuller's picture of Buchalter

Day in and day out, the contract killers sat in their usual booths, killing time with cards and craps while drinking steaming mugs of Rosie's famous malted milks. Once one of the payphones in the back began to ring, the member closest to the phone picked up and recorded the details of the next hit. The mobsters from the Syndicate would then send over a delegate who would take the hitman on a ride-along to case out the man or woman slated for assassination, allowing the hitman in question to memorize the target's appearance and be prepped about daily schedules and traveling routes.

Experts say the hitman's detachment to their targets was one of the key reasons behind the gang's longevity. Put simply, there was no emotion involved, just pure business. Still, this system was far from foolproof, as it led to a few cases of mistaken identity. 42-year-old classical music publishing executive Irving Penn, who supposedly "had not an enemy in the world," was mowed down by a troop of assassins driving by in a blue sedan in the late '30s. The hitmen had mistaken Penn for Philip Orlovsky, a labor union leader from the garment industry due to testify against Buchalter. But as damning as these incidents were to their reputation, such mistakes were few and far between. The hitmen adhered to a standard operating procedure – much of which was crafted by Bugsy – designed not only to eliminate targets efficiently, but to sever all ties between a hitman and their crimes. Following the order of a hit, a car was first stolen and concealed in a remote garage. A license plate was then prised off another vehicle and transferred to the stolen car. The "hot" car was then utilized during the assignment, along with a "trailing car," its purpose to slam into or obstruct police vehicles from catching up to the former vehicle. The hitmen were also instructed to acquire new weapons and to dispose of them immediately after they had been discharged. The "hot" cars, along with any other incriminating evidence (and at times, even the bodies) were also to be devoured by flames.

Bugsy, along with many other members of Murder, Inc., justified their horrendous actions by asserting, "We only kill each other." The hard-bitten practicality of this principle was most clearly demonstrated with the assassination of Arthur Flegenhemier, better known as "Dutch Schultz," who wasn't only one of their own, but one of the seemingly invulnerable founding fathers of the Syndicate. In 1935, Schultz found himself squirming under the microscope of special prosecutor and future governor of New York, Thomas E. Dewey. Schultz had been federally indicted for tax evasion, but even after he managed to shake off the charge, Dewey, who would most famously not defeat Harry Truman in the presidential election of 1948, refused to back off. In the public eye, Schultz appeared unruffled and dismissed the "rumors" about his criminal enterprises with the utmost nonchalance, but behind closed doors, it was a different story. Schultz, who reigned as the "Beer Baron of the Bronx" during the Prohibition Era, had everything to lose. Apart from the multiple labor unions he controlled and the $2 million a year he pulled in from harassing restaurant owners for "protection fees," his numbers racket in Harlem alone was netting $35,000 a day.

Dewey

The nearly inconsolable Schultz demanded that the squad terminate Dewey at once. Schultz's peers attempted to reason with him, citing the unwanted attention and other dangers that would result from such a brazen attack, but even after he was outvoted by Syndicate board members, he did not calm down. Bugsy, along with Lansky, Lucky, Costello, and Adonis, could only shoot knowing glances at one another when the exasperated Schultz flounced out of the room, but not before announcing that he would take matters into his own hands. This outburst was to board members more than enough proof that Schultz was a liability, one that had to be perpetually put to rest for the good of the Syndicate and all its divisions. And so, on the 24th of October, 1935, two men from Murder, Inc. crept into the Palace Chop House at 12 East Park Street in Newark and shot Schultz below the heart. Schultz limped out of the bathroom, clutching the wound below his heart, and plopped himself down on the table to die, but he was soon found and bussed off to the hospital, where he died 22 hours later.

Though it was supposedly Bugsy who insisted that he only killed those who made a living on the wrong side of the law, he did not always practice what he preached. When Lucky found himself tossed behind bars due to the testimony of a single snitch, Bugsy alone was hired to "take care" of the problem. Bugsy executed the target a few days later, but he was apparently spotted by a passing young woman. Rather than shuffle off with her head down, the woman made the mistake of approaching Bugsy and vehemently soliciting payment in exchange for her silence. The woman eventually bit her tongue and turned on her heel, but it was too late; Bugsy hauled her into the alley kicking and screaming, and raped her. He then concluded the horrific encounter with a threat, telling her that if she dared breathe a word about any of this, he would melt off her face with a bucket of acid.

By the late 1930s, Bugsy was increasingly restless about his position, so he passed the torch to Buchalter to focus on different projects with Lansky. Nonetheless, the exceptional marksman's services continued to be sought out by the higher-ups of the Syndicate. Lansky appeared to be the first among the pair to dive into the casino industry, but Bugsy soaked up every trick of the trade. They had come a long way from fleecing drunks and gamblers on the sidewalks, and their reputation in the field was now sacred. They were universally recognized for their "scrupulous honesty" and "vicious territoriality." When it came to casinos, Lansky prided himself on providing to his customers games that were "100% straight," for not only were profits comparable to fixed games, his casinos' unblemished record ensured that his tables were always full.

Bugsy, whose strong suit lay not in academics, but in street smarts, was tasked with patrolling the borders of their territory, keeping the prying law enforcement officials content and bringing down any potential competition. Obviously, violence was a given when it came to his line of work, but the connections that Lansky and Bugsy had developed with local authorities were so profound that he never received more than a slap on the wrist, if one could even call it that. On the 28th of February, 1932, Bugsy's 26th birthday, he was detained for having started a territorial tussle and inflicting grievous bodily harm on the other party, but he was charged only with "vagrancy" and made to shell out a $100 fine, which he footed by pulling out a crisp bill from the roll of $100 bills in his front pocket.

Another reason Lansky and Bugsy persevered for as long as they did was their sagacity, especially when it came to conjuring up various ways to take down their opponents without violence. The pair, for example, was aware that Waxey Gordon was committing the cardinal sin in the business by neglecting to launder his money through offshore accounts so as not to leave a trail, and in 1933, they leaked this tidbit to the IRS.

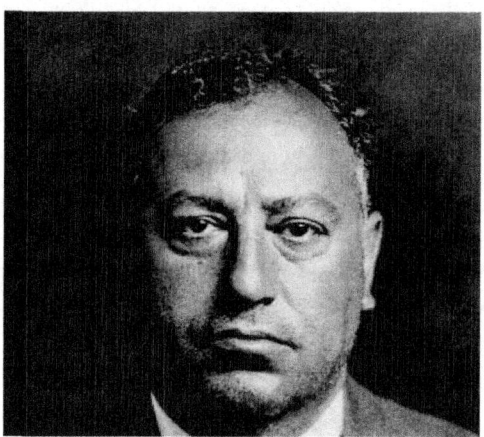

A mugshot of Gordon

Gordon, who was subsequently convicted for tax evasion, retaliated with an assassination attempt directed towards Bugsy and Lansky. Francis "Tony" Fabrizzo and his two brothers, Louis and Andy, were selected to execute the daring plot. Come the day of the assassination, the brothers tethered a cluster of dynamite to a piece of rope and lowered the explosives through the chimney of Bugsy and Lansky's office. The ever-observant Bugsy, however, caught sight of the bomb at once, and without so much as a second thought, Bugsy snipped off the bomb and hurled it out the window in the nick of time. The bomb exploded in mid-air, tearing off a chunk of the office wall and spraying shrapnel and debris in all directions, but Bugsy and Lansky were otherwise unharmed.

Their response was as swift as it was deadly. Bugsy checked himself into the hospital later that day to treat the scrapes, burns, and other superficial wounds he had sustained during the explosion. He then slipped out of his room unnoticed, met up with two other associates, and tracked down Louis and Andy Fabrizzo, offing them both in the same evening.

Not long after the demise of his brothers, Tony Fabrizzo revealed his intentions to write a memoir that would include a comprehensive chapter on Murder, Inc., and Bugsy's other illicit businesses. Tony, who Gordon regarded as his "top hitman," may have very well been on track to take down the legendary Bugsy Siegel, had it not been for his loose lips. About an hour or so after word had gotten to Bugsy, he checked himself into another hospital, and along with the same two accomplices, they dropped in on Tony by posing as detectives. The groggy Tony was shot dead before he could even step out onto his porch. Bugsy and his accomplices then parted ways, with the former furtively returning to his private room in the hospital. When authorities eventually came knocking on his door to investigate the murders of the Fabrizzo brothers, Bugsy was rendered untouchable by his air-tight alibis, complete with witnesses, which placed him in the hospital both evenings. Or so he thought.

Bugsy suffered no delusions about his unorthodox profession, and he always assumed it would only be a matter of time before his luck turned. When he learned about the holes in his alibis and the rapidly rising number of hits put out on him by vindictive mobsters, the Syndicate sent him to Los Angeles sometime in 1937, where he would remain until future notice. Bugsy was slightly disgruntled by having to relocate, but he was grateful when it came to the familiarity of the destination. As early as 1933, he had been traveling to the West Coast upon the Syndicate's request, including stints in California, where he was instructed to expand upon the organization's gambling rackets there, then overseen by the Los Angeles Black Hander, Jack Dragna.

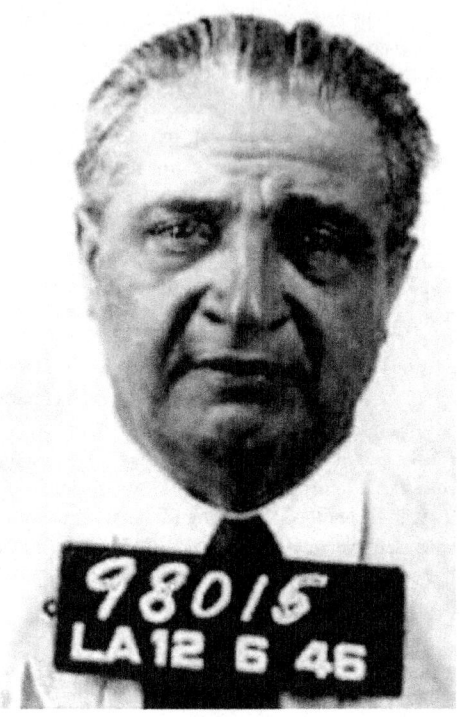

Dragna

Once Bugsy was all settled in, he rolled up his sleeves and proceeded to dethrone Dragna, selecting Mickey Cohen as his chief lieutenant. Dragna was more than displeased by the abrupt loss of prestige, but having been warned by Lucky and Lansky that it was "in his best interests to cooperate," he stepped aside, no questions asked, and allowed Bugsy to spearhead the Los Angeles numbers racket. Bugsy also used his expertise in the drug arena to design a trade route for narcotics between the United States and Mexico, a project that was sponsored by the Syndicate. On top of all that, Bugsy and Cohen co-founded their own race wire service, *Trans-America*. That said, rumor has it that Bugsy eventually started his own side hustle behind Cohen's back, dishonestly acquiring race results with the aid of "high-powered binoculars" and paying thugs to beat on Cohen's bookies.

Cohen

At the end of the day, the numbers racket in the City of Angels, say Bugsy's biographers, only continued to blossom, thanks to the seeds planted by Bugsy's guidance. By 1942, the Syndicate's bookmaking wire operations were reeling in approximately $500,000 a day.

Other Business Interests

Perhaps not surprisingly, the extent of Lansky's involvement in the crimes perpetrated by the mob is heavily contested, particularly by his surviving family members. They maintain that Lansky was no more than a mid-level financial manager-turned-scapegoat for Lucky's schemes. Conversely, they insist that Lansky was merely a driven individual who would soon become a gambling magnate in his own right. Perhaps those who have yet to be persuaded about the true depths of Lansky's alleged crimes have trouble believing that a family man as gentle and loving as he was could be capable of such callous and remorseless barbarism.

Others question how he was able to juggle both the competitiveness of the illicit booze market and a new family. In the spring of 1929, Lansky, then 27, tied the knot with one Anna Citron, with Bugsy serving as his best man. Lansky repaid the favor when Bugsy married Esther shortly after. Lansky and Anna went on to have three children, Buddy, Paul, and Sandra (or "Sandi").

It's possible that Lanky's growing family compelled him to become more audacious in his efforts to provide for his loved ones, especially since Buddy was diagnosed with cerebral palsy and required special care.

Following the demise of Prohibition in 1933, Lansky directed his focus to piecing together a gambling empire of his own. When Lucky ran out of his trademark good fortune three years later, Lansky was appointed the provisional director of his enterprises and was placed in charge of the operations' profits, as well as the personal finances of the disgraced mobster and his cronies. Sally Denton and Roger Morris, the authors of *The Making of Las Vegas and Its Hold on America 1947-2000,* explained the reasoning behind Lucky's decision: "For Luciano and other gangsters, [Lansky] was the preeminent investment banker and broker, a classic manager and financier of a growing multi-ethnic confederation of legal and illegal enterprises throughout the nation. He organized crime along corporate hierarchical lines, delineated authority and responsibility, holdings and subsidiaries, and most important, meticulously distributed shares of profits and proceeds, bonuses and prerequisites...In business, he preferred to own men more than property, especially public officials whose complicity was essential. He did not, like most of his associates, merely bribe politicians or policemen, but worked a more subtle, lasting venality, bringing them in as partners..."

At this juncture, Lansky had more than proven himself to be an artful entrepreneur with a sound business acumen. By 1936, he was operating a chain of "semi-legal" casinos in upstate New York, as well as New Orleans and southern Florida, and he set the =cornerstone of what would soon be a cardinal and highly remunerative relationship with Cuba. These "carpet joints," defined as the "ubiquitous casinos of the era," often had austere facades, but exquisitely decorated, carpeted interiors brimming with just about every game imaginable. Lansky had also purchased and strengthened a network of racetracks in Hallendale, Florida that raced dogs and horses. All the while, he continued to uphold his zero tolerance policy against swindling his customers, for he understood that the odds were forever in the house's favor. This ensured his establishments were superior to fraudulent "clip joints."

According to numerous biographers, it was towards the mid-1930s that Lansky applied for an offshore bank account in Switzerland to house his dirty cash, having been thoroughly spooked by Al Capone's 1931 conviction for tax evasion and pimping. Maintaining a Swiss account was to Lansky the obvious choice, owing to the 1934 Swiss Banking Act, which guaranteed all account owners absolute anonymity.

Apart from Bugsy, several ex-members of the Bugs and Meyer Mob, including Lansky's brother Jacob, Humie Siegel, Philip Kovolick, and Harry Stromberg, were incorporated into his fast ballooning empire. Lansky also collaborated with members of the Kid Cann Mob, headed by Isadore Blumenfield, former cohorts from the Prohibition years. The Blumenfield crew had granted patronage to quite a few of Lansky's first solo ventures, and even secured swathes of land along Miami Beach, which would become home to some of his upcoming hotels.

By 1935, following the immutable silencing of the dangerously impetuous Dutch Schultz, Lansky, among five others, was vilified by authorities as the most powerful operator of numbers rackets in Newark, Brooklyn, and Manhattan, and perhaps the entire East Coast. Still, what Lansky had built at this point would pale in comparison to his future endeavors in Cuba.

Lansky reinvested his mounting profits from his gambling empire into a variety of new businesses, though many believed them to be no more than hollow shell and holding companies, making them money-laundering fronts. He had the *Lansky Food Corporation* in New Jersey, as well as *Krieg, Spector, and Citron,* which boasted three branches in Hoboken, Newark, and Jersey City. Other companies Lansky was reportedly involved in throughout the latter half of the 190s and the early 1940s included the *Emby Distributing Company*, the *Manhattan Simplex Distributing Company,* the *Panuth Real Estate Corporation*, and the *Rosepot Real Estate Corporation.* He also owned a 25% stake in a number of properties, including on 922 Lexington Avenue, as well as the intersection of Lexington and 73rd Street, and between Madison Avenue and 73rd Street.

An even lesser-known fact about Lansky's business portfolio was his involvement in the music industry. A devout fan of the arts in general, he was linked to the famous *Wurlitzer* company, parented by the Baldwin Piano Company, a Cincinnati-based distributor of imported German musical instruments. Lansky, along with Frank Costello, distributed leases for organs, jukeboxes, and so on, and rented them out to bars, restaurants, and other establishments of the like throughout the 1940s, and were rewarded $15, or a hefty 60% cut of every sale per week.

Lansky is often portrayed as a number-crunching polymath who felt most comfortable behind the scenes, which was true to a certain extent, but he also managed the front ends of his establishments with great panache. Lansky's grandson, Meyer II, elaborated on this in an interview with Tony Sokol of *Den of Geek*: "There was a part of him that was very outgoing and social...he liked to have some drinks and listen to music...he wanted the best. Carmen Miranda wouldn't play at one of his casinos in Florida, so he had to go over to Cuba, which wasn't that far, and come back that night to bring her these special maracas that she wanted. He went out of his way to please people."

In conjunction with that, despite his escalating net worth, there was a stark absence of decadence in Lansky's lifestyle. He remained humble, for the most part, his thirst for knowledge never abating. Those closest to him recalled his habit of jotting down vocabulary words and interesting factoids, as well as little reminders to look up the proper pronunciation of certain words when he had the time to spare. Notwithstanding his growing affluence, Lansky dressed in simple white-on-white ensembles, and plain, but high-quality silk shirts that lasted him decades, opting for a nice tie or bowtie as opposed to the gaudy jewelry and costly watches sported by his associates and others with wealth.

Operation Underworld

"I was a Jew and I felt for those Jews in Europe who were suffering. They were my brothers."
– attributed to Meyer Lansky

Following the cataclysmic attack on Pearl Harbor in December 1941, the American morale was profoundly shaken, to say the least. The destruction of the glorious SS *Normandie,* which once bore the title of the "Greatest Liner Ever," almost exactly two months later came as another devastating blow. On February 9, 1942, New York's Pier 88 was flooded with miserable spectators, watching as the flustered firefighters aimed their hoses at the blazing vessel to no avail. They attempted to combat the flames, but after five and a half torturous hours, the *Normandie* listed to its side and sunk to the bottom of the Hudson River.

The *Normandie* reigned as the largest "turbo-electric powered" ocean liner in the world for five years, measuring over 1,000 feet in length and weighing over 60,000 tons. This French-made behemoth, the first ever to achieve a "30 knot eastbound Atlantic crossing," was the exemplar of the era's ultra-modern shipbuilding technology. James Hinton of the *New York History Blog* described the majesty of the peerless vessel, writing, "Her first class passenger spaces were decorated in the trendiest Art Deco style and filled with luxuries. The radical new hull design, with a subsurface bulb beneath a clipper bow, and long, sweeping lines lent her previously untouched speeds while requiring far less fuel. She even had one of the earliest radar sets ever used by a commercial vessel, in order to improve the safety [of] her passengers."

Following France's declaration of war on Germany in September 1939, the *Normandie* was docked at Pier 88. The American Coast Guard was then tasked with interning and guarding the ship, along with its French crew, which was confined to the vessel. Only five days after the Pearl Harbor attack, the French crew was made to disembark, and the ship was seized because France had been occupied by the Nazis. The *Normandie* was then rebranded the USS *Lafayette,* and orders were given to transform the ocean liner into a troop transport.

Alas, the transformation of the luxury liner was hastened, and consequently, it was poorly executed. President Roosevelt was informed that the USS *Lafayette* would be up and running on the 14th of February, but the dimensions of the colossal vessel and the intricacies of its technology made it extremely challenging to accomplish such a feat. On the 6th of February, just three days before the blaze, the crestfallen crew admitted to their superiors that the transformation could not be completed in time, and they requested that the deadline be delayed for two more weeks. To their consternation, their proposal was rebuffed, meaning they were left with no choice but to cut corners in order to accelerate the progress of the conversion. The temporary workshops aboard the ships were shambolic, and the spaces were improperly cleaned, with tools strewn about and open flames left unattended.

Three days after the extension for the deadline was denied, a crewman named Clement Derrick made what was most likely the biggest blunder of his life. Brandishing a blowtorch, Derrick flicked away the sweat on his brow as he cleaved through a few beams in what was once the vessel's first-class dining hall. A spark from Derrick's blowtorch kindled one of the life preservers carelessly stacked up against the wall. These life preservers, packed with a type of highly flammable cork known as "kapok," burst into flames in just a matter of seconds.

As the crew had disabled the vessel's sprinkler system, the roaring flames spread unchecked. It took no more than 15 minutes for the local fire department to arrive at the scene, but their feeble hoses were no match for the flames running rampant on the ship. One civilian, Frank Trentacosta, died, and another 285 were either burned or rendered bedridden from smoke inhalation. The charred remnants of the ship were retrieved about a year later, but authorities were made to disassemble the vessel and sell it for scrap metal in 1946. It would take decades for another ocean liner to rival the size and the once unbeatable speed of the *Normandie.*

The SS *Normandie*

For years, some refused to accept the apparent facts behind what appeared to be a preventable tragedy, instead churning out their own conspiracy theories. Some say undercover German spies snuck aboard the ship and deliberately ignited a flammable agent. Others proposed that mutineer crewmen who had enough of the perilous working conditions set the ship ablaze in protest. Others concluded that it was not an act of arson committed by foreign enemies, but by villains in their own backyard. One of the masterminds, they say, was Meyer Lansky.

While Lansky's name is frequently mentioned in the theory, it is Lucky Luciano who is identified as the attack's brainchild. According to this theory, the restive Lucky was wasting away in his prison cell when he learned that the *Normandie* had been relocated to Pier 88, and it was then that he found an opportunity for early release. The following day, he summoned Lansky, Costello, and Moe Polakoff, and he disclosed to them his sophisticated, but wicked plans.

With that said, it wasn't until the morning after the Pearl Harbor disaster that the plan was put into effect. During visitation hours, Lucky pointed to an article from the day's newspaper giddily, and directed them towards a passage that detailed the navy's concerns about the safety of the harbor's ships against amphibious German forces. If they were to somehow sink the ship, Lucky mused, the U.S. Navy could do nothing but begrudgingly request the aid of the Luciano family and his valuable contacts. Then, Lucky continued, he could demand a pardon from the very man who threw him behind bars in the first place: prosecutor Thomas Dewey.

As temptingly plausible as this theory may sound, almost everyone considers this deleterious gossip. By all appearances, Lansky, while rough around the edges, was a fervent patriot who detested bigotry, discrimination, and everything the Nazis stood for. He was genuine in his war efforts, and more significantly, he would have never involved himself in such an imprudent, heinous act that would have put the lives of civilians – not to mention all that he had built – at risk.

Indeed, the casino baron, Lansky's chroniclers claim, had always been vehemently opposed to the bullying of minorities, particularly Jews. All throughout his life, he was known to fend off bullies with his own muscle, and he greatly opposed anti-Semites following the start of the Second World War. His vigilante endeavors were so effective that local authorities began to commission Lansky and his "security team" to "remedy" numerous relevant disputes.

When the chaotic German-American Bund rallies began to multiply in New York during the late 1930s, American Jewish officials were as enraged as they were conflicted. The German-American Bund, a white-only organization founded in 1936 to propagate the toxic ideals of Nazi Germany, was a disgusting affront to many, but it was perfectly legal. As odious as the convictions of these "Bundists" were, authorities had no right to disband them, nor were they vested with the power to quash their disturbing rallies.

However, one local judge, Justice Nathan Perlman, would stand for these poisonous displays no longer. As such, he reached out to Lansky and ordered his men to shut down the Bund rallies. Though Lansky was granted permission to exert force if need be, they were to restrain themselves from killing any Bundists, even if they were to attack first. Lansky agreed to all these stipulations, but he refused to accept compensation for what he deemed to be his civilian duty.

Lansky described one of the "Brown Shirt" rallies his men disrupted in the Yorkville area of Manhattan: "We got there that evening and found several hundred people dressed in brown shirts. The stage was decorated with a swastika and pictures of Hitler. The speaker started ranting. There were only about fifteen of us, but we went into action. We attacked them in the hall, and threw some of them out the windows. There were fistfights all over the place...Most of the Nazis panicked and ran out. We chased them and beat them up, and some of them were out of action for months. Yes, it was violence [sic]. We wanted to teach them a lesson. We wanted to show them that Jews would not always sit back and accept insults..."

Lansky's minions were always punctual, and they abided by a strict code of conduct, carrying out their shutdowns with "military precision." His agents were posted on both sides of the entrance and exits, for example, to ensure that no violent Bundits or Nazi sympathizers could escape unscathed.

It wasn't just Lansky's immaculate track record in dissolving these rallies that rendered his services so valuable. In fact, authorities turned to him because they were confident he would do precisely as he was instructed, albeit after indulging in some creative freedom. According to Lansky, "There were no killings or permanent injuries at these events...only dislocated limbs, bloodied heads and noses, and damage requiring dental work." Robert Rockaway confirmed this: "Nazi arms, legs, and ribs were broken, and skulls were cracked, but no one died."

It was apparently because of Lansky's anti-Nazi activism that the Navy enlisted his help in further securing the docks and its ships after the *Normandie* disaster. Furthermore, the 40-year-old gangster had offered his services to the U.S. Army as a member of the troops a few years prior, but he was rejected on account of his age and height.

On top of that, Lansky was passionate about politics, evidenced by the cash donations he allegedly contributed to Democratic campaigns over the years. As recorded by legal scholar William Chambliss, Lansky donated money to "the presidential campaigns of Al Smith (1928)...Franklin Roosevelt (1932)...Harry Truman (1948)...Lyndon Johnson (1960 & 1964)...[and] Hubert Humphrey (1968)."

More crucially, Lansky was a close confidante of Lucky's (the man they were truly after), and while he was allegedly a venerated figure in the underworld, his lack of a criminal record cemented the Navy's choice to use him as a mediator. One may also refer to this statement issued by an unidentified former official of the White House: "The dirty little secret of 'Operation Underworld' was that the United States government needed Lansky...and organized crime to force an industrial peace and a policing of sabotage on the wharves and in the warehouses. The government turned to him because hiring thugs was what government and business had been doing for a long time to control workers, and because it could conceive little other choice in the system at hand."

However it came about, on May 12, 1942, Lansky and a few delegates from the Navy journeyed up to the Clinton Correctional Facility, a maximum security prison based in Dannemora, New York. By the end of the negotiations, authorities had agreed to transfer Lucky to Comstock's Great Meadow Correctional Facility, where the rules were laxer and the amenities were far more fulfilling. Most appealing of all was the one-way ticket to Sicily they promised him following a drastic reduction of his 30-50 year maximum prison sentence.

Once the deal between both parties had been finalized, Lucky briefed Lansky on the plan of action and entrusted him with overseeing the covert operation. When Lansky and the Navy's representatives departed, Lucky seated himself before a payphone and began ringing up all his contacts, near and far. The planting of spies in areas heavily populated with Bundists and other Nazi partisans, such as Yorkville, was the most critical component of the operation. Lucky's agents, disguised as cigarette and hatcheck girls, bathroom attendants, prostitutes, and bartenders lingered in Bundist bars, strategically snooped on multiple conversations all at once. "Numbers runners," as well as those employed to maintain vending machines around the city, were also made to eavesdrop and keep track of the Bundist leaders' every movement.

All this unconventional investigative work finally paid off when one of Lucky's informants tipped the authorities off on a Nazi submarine loitering by the docks in Long Island, where the Germans often unloaded their own spies. Once authorities received this intelligence, they swooped in on the submarine and captured a total of eight German spies, six of whom were later executed for conspiring to poison the water supply and destroy a variety of defenses with bombs. Both Lucky and Lansky are also said to have provided photographs of the Sicilian coastline, as well as detailed maps of the city and the numbers of priceless contacts in the region, which allowed for the Allies' smooth invasion of Sicily in 1943. As pledged by the authorities, Lucky was paroled in 1946 and quietly deported to Sicily, thereby serving only a fraction of his full sentence.

For the next four decades or so, the American government dodged questions about the controversial Operation Underworld, unwilling to credit the mobsters for their indispensable assistance. The inquiries about reports outlining Lansky's contributions to naval campaigns, such as the security he provided for both active U.S. warships and vessels under construction, fell on deaf ears. Corresponding records also stated that Lansky, with the aid of his associate Louis Lepke, investigated and discontinued the efforts of Bundists and Nazis attempting to blow up chemical plants, industrial factories, railroads, synagogues, and Jewish establishments in Manhattan.

Lansky's patriotism apparently did not stop there. Some say Lansky and Lucky once concocted a devious plan that would have most likely terminated the war several years earlier: the assassinations of Adolf Hitler and Benito Mussolini. The pair were prepared to part with what was probably millions for Vito Genovese of the Genovese Crime Family to enforce the executions. When they approached Genovese about the assignment in late July of 1943, however, Mussolini had already been ejected from his seat of power. Additionally, much to their chagrin, Genovese had no interest whatsoever in offing Hitler, since this would likely bring about the conclusion of the war and the dissolution of the thriving black market. That said, as intriguing as this story may be, there is little proof to support it.

In the end, many of Lansky's biographers claim that he took great offense to the American government's refusal to honor his achievements. He did not care for compensation, nor did he expect to be awarded a glittering medal, but the tremendous effort they put into dissembling the facts did not sit well with him. Whether he believed it or not, to the government, he bore the indelible stamp of a contemptible criminal.

Lansky's Twilight

"You never want to build something when you don't own the land underneath it." – attributed to Lansky by his grandson

Towards the latter half of the 1940s, the decaying marriage between Lansky and Anne finally crumbled, leading to their divorce in early 1947. A few months later, while vacationing in Miami, Lansky made the acquaintance of Thelma "Teddy" Sheer, a quick-witted, curly-haired woman five years his junior. It would not take long for Lansky to fall head over heels for Teddy, who was strong-willed, but affectionate and fiercely devoted. Lansky soon proposed, and the pair were married by the following year.

The trust that Teddy had in her husband was unparalleled, for throughout the entirety of their 35-year marriage, not once did she inquire about the source of his bread and butter. She knew practically nothing about her husband's enterprises, or so she claimed. Perhaps Lansky wanted it that way, figuring that the less his loved ones knew, the better.

According to multiple interviews featuring Lansky's relatives, the couple appeared to have a healthy, loving relationship, and they were highly respected by members of their communities, aside from local authorities. Judy Gretah, Teddy's granddaughter from a previous marriage, described them as "very quiet people" who lived life by routine. Lansky's step-granddaughter, Cynthia Duncan, remembered, "My grandfather was a really nice guy. In restaurants, people would come up to the dinner table very respectful, like he was a god. Some came to him and asked, 'Can you loan me some money for my son's bar mitzvah?'" It was a request that was almost always generously fulfilled.

Following the end of the Second World War, Lansky resumed with the expansion of his ever-growing gambling empire, soon owning "points casinos" in Las Vegas, London, Cuba, and the Bahamas. Not only was Lansky an expert in selecting games that provided the house with the best (but fair) odds, he continued to reinforce his relationships with bribes, as well as the implementation of various favors. In order to stave off suspicion, county officials on Lansky's payroll proceeded with identifying transgressions committed by his corporations and charging them for these said offenses, but all would be conveniently settled by court fines.

An excerpt from an article entitled "Lansky: The Godfather of Money Laundering," by Paul Camacho spelled out the understanding between both parties: "Municipal court records show a dramatic increase in civil fines that coincide with the establishment of a Lansky operation. It seems the same group of Lansky associates were charged repeatedly for disorderly conduct, but none ever made their court appearance...allowing the assessment of a hefty nonappearance fine."

It was during this time that Bugsy approached Lansky, requesting that he put in a good word for him regarding the takeover of the Las Vegas gambling scene. Lansky succeeded in doing just that, but he did more than just vouch for his longtime comrade. Ultimately, he became one of the principal investors in the Flamingo. In late 1945, Lansky and the rest of the investors purchased the land required for the construction site and received a 2/3 stake in the property. Some sources claim that the Flamingo, soon to be marketed as the most phenomenal hotel-casino in all of Vegas, was actually Lansky's vision, not Bugsy's, but there exists little proof to support this claim. Either way, Lansky was thrilled by the potential profits they were certain to amass in Nevada, where casinos were legalized in 1931.

K. Stadelman's picture of the Flamingo

Unfortunately for the mobsters, Bugsy quickly appeared to be out of his depth, his grandiose visions for the 105-room property pairing dismally with his impetuous spending habits. The Flamingo was scheduled to open its doors in early December 1946, but the grand opening was pushed back due to outstanding bills, as well as lack of management. The hotel-casino finally opened its doors the day after Christmas, but it was shut down again shortly thereafter when incomplete repairs came to light.

The mafioso investors were understandably irate by Bugsy's failure to hold down the fort, and some of them held a conference in Havana, Cuba to address these problems. The better part of those present demanded that Bugsy be killed for his sins, but Lansky, as the story goes, implored them to humor Bugsy with a second chance. Following the meeting, Lansky returned to Las Vegas and sternly reprimanded Bugsy, ordering him to clean up his act. Bugsy didn't heed Lansky's warnings, which resulted in a second conference, but by the time of that meeting, Bugsy had managed to produce a small, but notable profit, which Lansky relied on to spare the life of his friend once more.

Eventually, the Flamingo began to hemorrhage cash once again, now at an even more alarming rate. A third and final meeting was held, and Lansky pleaded again on Bugsy's behalf, but he ultimately had to accept Bugsy's dark inescapable fate. On June 20, 1947, Bugsy was mowed down by a hail of bullets in the living room of the house of his girlfriend, Virginia Hall. Just a mere 20 minutes after Bugsy's death, Moe Sedway and Gus Greenbaum marched into the Flamingo, allegedly uprooting Bugsy's flag and replacing it with Lansky's. As maintained by the FBI, Lansky's substantial shares in the Flamingo were preserved for the next two decades. Control of the Vegas gambling scene was eventually transferred to Chicago mob boss Tony Accardo, a transition supposedly coordinated by Lansky.

Inevitably, the extent of Lansky's involvement in Bugsy's murder continues to be a matter of dispute. Some say it was Lansky himself who consigned Bugsy to death after unearthing the $2.5 million that Bugsy allegedly embezzled from the Flamingo. Others, in particular Lansky's family members, assert that Lansky was no more than a lowly financier of the hotel-casino, and that he had nothing to do with preventing or conducting the murder.

Interestingly enough, Lansky's own daughter, Sandi, had a different theory. It was never about the money, insisted Sandi, but the irreverence Bugsy exhibited to Lucky Luciano one fateful evening after showing up late to a meeting. As with so much surrounding the mobsters, nobody can be certain.

Lansky soon bade good riddance to Las Vegas, for the razzle-dazzle of Sin City had revealed itself to be no more than cheap confetti and tawdry pageantry. Quite Frankly, it proved to be more trouble than it was worth. Lansky said, "There were times when I thought I would die in that desert. Vegas was a horrible place."

As fate would have it, that was only the beginning of the legal, mental, and physical troubles that would befall Lansky. In the early 1950s, he found himself targeted by the Kefauver Committee, a group put together by the U.S. Senate to crack down on organized crime. A number of the witnesses subpoenaed were linked to the usually discreet Lansky, who was consequently summoned to court on three different occasions. Despite the dearth of proof presented, he was labeled as a powerful leader of an "East Coast Crime Syndicate."

Lansky was eventually released uncharged, but this brush with justice was far too close of a call. He fought tooth and nail to legitimize his gambling enterprises in the United States the best he could, only to have his wings clipped by what he thought to be unjust restrictions and illogical laws. It no longer made sense to house his nerve center in the country.

In the mid-1950s, the dictator Fulgencio Batista invited Lansky to renovate and resuscitate Cuba's gambling landscape, a proposition that Lansky anxiously accepted. Given Havana's close proximity to Florida, Cuba flourished as the ultimate getaway spot for affluent American tourists, as this tropical paradise not only ignored, but almost welcomed the vices that were strictly outlawed in their country. During this time, however, Cuba was suffering a storm of backlash from American journalists who condemned the Caribbean's casinos as "clip joints." Lansky's job was to remodel the most popular casinos and racetracks in Cuba, and inject into them the integrity he had used to make his reputation. For his services, Lansky was reportedly paid $25,000 a year, minus his share of the profits, and by the end of the decade, Lansky's personal net worth was estimated to be around $16 or $17 million.

Ever the businessman, Lansky was eager to capitalize on the swelling casino market in Cuba, and he got behind a grand resort-casino of his own, one that would put the Flamingo to shame. The titanic project was to set Lansky and the investors back $19 million, but the end result would clearly be worth every penny. On December 10, 1957, a blinding cast of cinematic legends, Hollywood starlets, arena-playing musicians, and other members of the social elite entered the Havana Riviera for the first time. Visitors, greeted by the soothing chill of the air-conditioning (the first of its kind to be equipped with such a feature), marveled at the pristine mosaic floors, satin curtains, and what appeared to be about every game in existence.

Again, the details of Lansky's ownership are blurred. While some have reduced his role to a silent partner, the general consensus is that Lansky had full ownership of the Riviera. To avoid further scrutiny, however, he supposedly declined to have any formal association with the resort-casino, thereby limiting the paper trail. Instead, he was listed only as the Riviera's "Director of Kitchen Operations."

Lansky's Cuban venture was a major success at its inception, but it soon became apparent that he had just made the worst decision of his career. Unlike with the Flamingo during its early years, the Riviera's failure was caused by external factors out of Lansky's hands. In 1958, revolutionary insurgents led by Fidel Castro commandeered the Riviera. Cutting his losses, Lansky hastily repacked his bags and fled Cuba the day before Castro reached Havana.

Lansky settled in Miami, where he hoped to live out the rest of his retirement in peace. Much to his exasperation, however, the authorities would allow no such thing. He was hounded by both journalists and law enforcement, who consistently crashed his grocery and dry-cleaning trips and badgered him with prying questions and accusations.

Sometime between the late 1950s and the early 1960s, authorities bugged his entire house, as well as the establishments he frequented, and began to tap all his incoming and outgoing phone calls. Such a tactic had proved successful in nabbing some of the most feared mobsters to ever come out of the United States, but with Lansky, they gathered absolutely zilch. Lansky, it seemed, spent his days lounging on the couch in front of the television, spending quality time with his family members and playing gin rummy with a close-knit group of friends and neighbors.

The only clue Lansky ever provided that indicated his ties to the mob came out on May 27, 1962. While watching a program about American mobsters in his living room, Lansky is said to have uttered the following remark to Teddy: "Organized crime [in America] is bigger than U.S. Steel." Lansky was the muse for the antagonist Hyman Roth in *The Godfather II,* and thus he was the source for the movie's famous quote: "Michael, we're bigger than US Steel."

On October 28, 1969, while relaxing in the steam room of the Doral Beach Spa, Lansky was abruptly served with a summons to appear before a federal grand jury. He was accused of skimming profits from the Flamingo, but he was eventually acquitted. Just four months later, Lansky was once again apprehended upon returning from a vacation to Acapulco by security officers, who discovered a vial of Donnatal tablets on him. Lansky claimed the tablets were to combat his bleeding stomach ulcers, but when he failed to produce evidence of the prescription, he was promptly arrested.

His arrest was sensationalized by numerous publications the following morning, among them the *Miami Herald*: "Lansky was taken to the Miami Strike Force offices where he was fingerprinted and charged with two indictments, one a felony, one a misdemeanor for possession of barbiturates and unlabeled drugs...The felony charge carried a two-year prison sentence and a fine of up to $1,000, the misdemeanor, six months in jail, and $500."

A criminal court judge ultimately dismissed the drug charges against him, but the hapless retiree quickly fell under scrutiny again, this time for tax evasion. Having had enough of the harassment, Lansky and Teddy moved to Israel in late July 1970 in hopes of gaining permanent citizenship, as per the Law of Return, which guaranteed citizenship to "all members of the Jewish people everywhere – be they living in poverty and fear of persecution, or in affluence and safety."

There, Lansky and Teddy were afforded a life of solitude and serenity for a short time. Jerry Klinger of *The Jewish Magazine* described a typical day in the life of the retiree: "He arose early, before 7AM, and took Bruiser [their shihtzu] for a walk along the waterfront. Returning to the hotel, he would enjoy [an] Israeli hotel smorgasbord breakfast of five types of herring, ten types of cheese and breads, salads to choose from...and various Middle Eastern pastries and hot dishes...He would sit and talk for hours about life in Israel, West Bank settlements, the Arab issues, Israeli politics, and the like in the hotel lobby over steaming pots of coffee and cigarettes..."

As soon as the American journalists tracked him down in Israel, Lansky's life of quiet came to a screeching halt. Up until this point, the Israeli Minister of Interior was prepared to grant Lansky the asylum he so desperately sought, but upon learning of Lansky's alleged ties to the mob, the Israelis rejected his application. Lansky reportedly offered as many as seven countries – Argentina, Brazil, Switzerland, Bolivia, Peru, Paraguay, and Panama – a whopping $1 million in exchange for citizenship, but none would take him up on his offer.

As a result, Lansky returned to Miami on November 7, 1972. "That's life," was Lansky's comment to the rabble of reporters. "At my age, it's too late to worry. What will be will be. A Jew has a slim chance in this world." Lansky was apprehended, cuffed, and booked just minutes after his landing, but he posted the $250,000 bail assigned to his case and was released later that same day. The media ran countless stories surrounding Lansky, whom they dubbed the "Gangland Finance Chairman" and the "reputed financial genius of the underworld," but a Miami jury ultimately cleared him all of charges.

Once more, celebrations were short-lived, for he was indicted again on related tax evasion charges in late 1973. According to "Fat Vinnie" Teresa, a well-known police informant, he once delivered to Lansky his share of the profits for one of his casinos in London, a sum intentionally left out come tax season. Yet again, Lansky was acquitted, in large part thanks to the testimony of his wife, Teddy, who presented receipts proving that Lansky had been undergoing surgery for his hernia on the day of the supposed delivery.

The detectives and prosecutors who spent decades assembling cases against Lansky were understandably incensed by their inability to keep him behind bars. One FBI agent admitted that he never came to terms with the fact that Lansky had outsmarted them, "laughing that he whipped us all." Another reflected about what Lansky could have been, noting he "would have been chairman of the board of General Motors if he'd gone into legitimate business."

While so many prominent mobsters met fates similar to Bugsy's, Lansky's death was relatively peaceful. On January 15, 1983, he died in Mount Sinai Hospital in New York due to complications from lung cancer. He was 81.

Precisely just how much Lansky was worth is a topic that continues to be hotly debated to this day. Journalists insisted that the he had hoarded up to $300 million in various Swiss bank accounts, whereas others claimed he had no more than between $10,000 and $35,000 to his name at the time of his death, having spent the bulk of his fortune on his failed venture in Cuba and the defenses for his multiple trials. In fact, Lansky was apparently so broke that he could not provide for his disabled son, Buddy, who lived the rest of his adulthood in destitution.

Lansky's relatives, such as his step-granddaughter Cynthia, tell a different story. It was Sandi, Cynthia asserted, who stole Buddy's inheritance, leaving him penniless until his death in 1989. And while they deny all knowledge of Lansky's phantom millions, Cynthia claims that Lansky had indeed left a humble fortune, among which included a $50,000 certificate of deposit stowed away in a laundry basket, as well as an assortment of jewelry.

As any biography of Lansky has to concede, it will likely never be possible to fully understand his life, but his story may be best summed up by one of his own quotes: "When you lose your money, you lose nothing; when you lose your health, you lose something; when you lose your character, you lose everything..."

Online Resources

Other books about gangsters by Charles River Editors

Other books about Meyer Lansky on Amazon

Further Reading

Editors, B. *Meyer Lansky Biography*. 2 Apr. 2014, www.biography.com/people/meyer-lansky-9542634. Accessed 3 Sept. 2018.

McPadden, M. *MEYER LANSKY: 5 KILLER FACTS ABOUT THE MOB'S NOTORIOUS MONEY MAN*. 13 Dec. 2017, crimefeed.com/2017/12/meyer-lansky-5-killer-facts-about-the-mobs-most-notorious-money-man/. Accessed 3 Sept. 2018.

Editors, F P. *Meyer Lansky Biography*. 7 Apr. 2018, www.thefamouspeople.com/profiles/meyer-lansky-8965.php. Accessed 3 Sept. 2018.

Fishel, H. *Meyer Lansky – The American Jewish Mobster Who Hunted Down Nazi Sympathizers And Secured New York Harbor*. 13 Dec. 2017, www.warhistoryonline.com/world-war-ii/meyer-lansky-the-american.html. Accessed 3 Sept. 2018.

Editors, S F. *Interesting Facts About Meyer Lansky*. 2018, thestickyfacts.com/meyer-lansky-facts/. Accessed 3 Sept. 2018.

Sokol, T. *Making of the Mob: Meyer Lansky's Grandson Testifies*. 16 June 2015, www.denofgeek.com/us/tv/the-making-of-the-mob-new-york/246986/making-of-the-mob-meyer-lansky-s-grandson-testifies. Accessed 3 Sept. 2018.

Radeska, T. *Things You Might Not Know about Meyer Lansky, the Mafia Financier and Math Genius*. 27 Sept. 2016, www.thevintagenews.com/2016/09/27/things-might-not-know-meyer-lansky-mafia-financier-math-genius/. Accessed 3 Sept. 2018.

Editors, A G. *SO A NAZI WALKS INTO AN IRON BAR: THE MEYER LANSKY STORY*. 22 Feb. 2017, www.anarchogeekreview.com/history/so-a-nazi-walks-into-an-iron-bar-the-meyer-lansky-story. Accessed 3 Sept. 2018.

Welkos, R W. *Meyer Lansky's Mafia Secrets Exposed By Daughter*. 21 May 2010, www.fivefamiliesnyc.com/2010/05/meyer-lanskys-mafia-secrets-exposed-by.html. Accessed 3 Sept. 2018.

Bellucci, D. *MEYER LANSKY – MAFIA ASSASSIN – MURDER INCORPORATED – RUSSIAN JEWISH MAFIA*. 26 Nov. 2012, dagobertobellucci.wordpress.com/2012/11/26/meyer-lansky-mafia-assassin-murder-incorporated-russian-jewish-mafia/. Accessed 3 Sept. 2018.

Editors, W G. *Boardwalk Empire Profile: Meyer Lansky Timeline*. 25 Oct. 2010, whiskeygoldmine.com/downtown-bar-stories-lounge-club/boardwalk-empire-hbo-prohibition-gangster-mafia-mob/boardwalk-empire-profile-meyer-lansky-lucky-luciano-arnold-rothstein-nucky-thompson-bugsy-segal-jewish-commission-prohibition-syndicate-mob-boss-gambling-drugs-heroin-wwii-vegas-cuba-riviera-flamingo/. Accessed 3 Sept. 2018.

Editors, M M. *MEYER LANSKY*. 2017, themobmuseum.org/notable_names/meyer-lansky/. Accessed 3 Sept. 2018.

Dean, H. *Meyer Lansky: Died On This Day in 1983, Aged 80*. 31 July 2018, www.nationalcrimesyndicate.com/on-this-day-in-1983-meyer-lansky-died/. Accessed 3 Sept. 2018.

Ferrara, E. *MEYER LANSKY'S NEW YORK: A GUIDE*. 2017, www.leshp.org/blog/meyer-lansky-new-york-guide/. Accessed 3 Sept. 2018.

von Lampe, K. *Little Man: Meyer Lansky and the Gangster Life*. 2010, www.organized-crime.de/revlac01.htm. Accessed 3 Sept. 2018.

Bullough, M. *The Downfall of the Havana Mob*. 21 Feb. 2010, in1959.blogspot.com/2010/02/downfall-of-havana-mob.html. Accessed 3 Sept. 2018.

Editors, Q C. *Meyer Lansky Quotes*. 2017, quotecatalog.com/communicator/meyer-lansky/. Accessed 3 Sept. 2018.

Pelaia, A. *A Profile of Meyer Lansky*. 26 May 2017, www.thoughtco.com/who-was-meyer-lansky-2076722. Accessed 4 Sept. 2018.

Editors, M L. *BIOGRAPHY*. 2016, www.officialmeyerlansky.com/bio.php. Accessed 4 Sept. 2018.

Klinger, J. *In Search of Meyer*. Feb. 2009, www.jewishmag.com/130mag/meyer_lansky/meyer_lansky.htm. Accessed 4 Sept. 2018.

Editors, N Y. *MEYER LANSKY IS DEAD AT 81; FINANCIAL WIZARD OF ORGANIZED CRIME*. 16 Jan. 1983, www.nytimes.com/1983/01/16/obituaries/meyer-lansky-is-dead-at-81-financial-wizard-of-organized-crime.html. Accessed 4 Sept. 2018.

Denton, S, and R Morris. *The Money and the Power The Making of Las Vegas and Its Hold on America, 1947-2000* . 2001, archive.nytimes.com/www.nytimes.com/books/first/d/denton-power.html. Accessed 4 Sept. 2018.

Meyer, D. *Meyer Lansky - Gangster and Gambler*. 2014, www.j-grit.com/criminals-meyer-lansky-gangster-and-gambler.php. Accessed 4 Sept. 2018.

Editors, M H. *Meyer Lansky*. 2017, www.mafia-history.org/gangsters/meyer-lansky.php. Accessed 4 Sept. 2018.

Editors, C M. *Meyer Lansky*. 2017, www.crimemuseum.org/crime-library/organized-crime/meyer-lansky/. Accessed 4 Sept. 2018.

Editors, R. *The Bugs and Meyer Mob*. 19 June 2018, www.revolvy.com/page/The-Bugs-and-Meyer-Mob. Accessed 4 Sept. 2018.

Harvey, I. *Lucky Luciano Started His Own Gang as a Teenager and Became the New York Mafia's Boss of Bosses*. 14 Feb. 2017, www.thevintagenews.com/2017/02/14/charles-lucky-luciano-started-his-own-gang-as-a-teenager-and-became-the-new-york-mafias-boss-of-bosses/. Accessed 4 Sept. 2018.

Mendel, N. *Rabbi Meir*. 11 Nov. 2010, www.chabad.org/library/article_cdo/aid/112312/jewish/Rabbi-Meir.htm. Accessed 4 Sept. 2018.

Haller, M H. *Lansky, Meyer*. 2009, www.anb.org/view/10.1093/anb/9780198606697.001.0001/anb-9780198606697-e-2001524. Accessed 4 Sept. 2018.

Zipperstein, S J. *The Long Roots of Russian Anti-Semitism*. 30 May 2018, www.newstatesman.com/culture/books/2018/05/long-roots-russian-anti-semitism. Accessed 4 Sept. 2018.

Helgeson, J. *American Labor and Working-Class History, 1900–1945*. 2017, americanhistory.oxfordre.com/view/10.1093/acrefore/9780199329175.001.0001/acrefore-9780199329175-e-330. Accessed 4 Sept. 2018.

Editors, B. *History of Wages in the United States from Colonial Times to ... United States*. 4 Feb. 2018, babel.hathitrust.org/cgi/pt?id=uc1.32106007458745;view=1up;seq=291. Accessed 4 Sept. 2018.

Editors, R. *Broadway Mob*. 30 May 2017, www.revolvy.com/page/Broadway-Mob. Accessed 5 Sept. 2018.

Editors, I M. *Meyer Lansky*. 2012, sites.google.com/site/mafiaprohibition/meyer-lansky. Accessed 5 Sept. 2018.

Editors, A I. *GANGSTERS DURING PROHIBITION*. 2007, webpage.pace.edu/pp31462n/prohibition/gangsters.html. Accessed 5 Sept. 2018.

Editors, G I. *How Mob Boss Meyer Lansky Laundered the American Mafia's Dirty Cash – and Made Them Bigger than U.S. Steel*. 25 May 2016, gangstersinc.ning.com/profiles/blogs/how-meyer-lansky-laundered-the-american-mafia-s-dirty-cash-and-ma. Accessed 5 Sept. 2018.

Editors, J V. *Arnold Rothstein*. 2017, www.jewishvirtuallibrary.org/arnold-rothstein. Accessed 5 Sept. 2018.

Bradford, B. *Arnold Rothstein and Drugs*. 1 June 2016, barrybradford.com/arnold-rothstein/. Accessed 5 Sept. 2018.

Editors, G S. *Arnold Rothstein*. 2017, www.gamblingsites.org/biographies/arnold-rothstein/. Accessed 5 Sept. 2018.

Editors, B F. *Arnold Rothstein: He Helped Organize Organized Crime*. 2015, www.babyfacenelsonjournal.com/arnold-rothstein.html. Accessed 5 Sept. 2018.

James, E. *Arnold Rothstein – the Jewish Godfather of Organized Crime in America*. 27 Dec. 2015, eurofolkradio.com/2015/12/27/arnold-rothstein-the-jewish-godfather-of-organized-crime-in-america/. Accessed 5 Sept. 2018.

Editors, A M. *Salvatore Maranzano, and the Castellamarese War*. 6 Mar. 2014, americanmafiahistory.com/salvatore-maranzano/. Accessed 5 Sept. 2018.

Editors, N C. *How Did Salvatore Maranzano Get Killed? – Death Photos*. 2018, www.nationalcrimesyndicate.com/salvatore-maranzano-death/. Accessed 5 Sept. 2018.

Editors, N C. *Salvatore Maranzano – The Boss of Bosses*. 2018, www.nationalcrimesyndicate.com/salvatore-maranzano-the-boss-of-bosses/. Accessed 5 Sept. 2018.

Lansky II, M. *The Many Faces of Meyer Lansky*. 4 Feb. 2014, www.huffingtonpost.com/meyer-lansky-ii/the-many-faces-of-meyer-l_b_4579284.html. Accessed 5 Sept. 2018.

Editors, P B. *Meyer Lansky* . 2016, prabook.com/web/meyer.lansky/721756. Accessed 5 Sept. 2018.

Gage, N. *U. S. Investigating Lansky's Crime Web*. 10 June 1971, www.nytimes.com/1971/06/10/archives/us-investigating-lanskys-crime-web-us-is-investigating-lanskys-web.html. Accessed 6 Sept. 2018.

Editors, J V. *Jews in America: Jewish Gangsters*. 2016, www.jewishvirtuallibrary.org/jewish-gangsters-in-america. Accessed 6 Sept. 2018.

Ray, R. *19 Mobsters Historically Tied to Gambling*. 6 May 2017, www.gamblingsites.com/blog/19-mobsters-historically-tied-to-gambling-24729/. Accessed 6 Sept. 2018.

Francis, S. *The Managerial Mob*. 12 Mar. 2018, www.chroniclesmagazine.org/the-managerial-mob/. Accessed 6 Sept. 2018.

Editors, I N. *Posts Tagged 'Broadway Mob.'* 2018, infamousnewyork.com/tag/broadway-mob/. Accessed 6 Sept. 2018.

Editors, W G. *What Is a Mustache Pete?* 2011, www.wisegeek.com/what-is-a-mustache-pete.htm. Accessed 6 Sept. 2018.

Hinton, J. *The Sinking of The S.S. Normandie At NYC's Pier 88*. 23 Sept. 2014, Editors, W G. What Is a Mustache Pete? 2011, www.wisegeek.com/what-is-a-mustache-pete.htm. Accessed 6 Sept. 2018. Accessed 6 Sept. 2018.

Grace, M L. *Cruise Ship History: The French Line's SS NORMANDIE. The Greatest Liner Ever to Sail "across the Pond"! Will the SS United States and QE 2 Face a Similar Demise?* 18 Feb. 2009, www.cruiselinehistory.com/cruise-ship-history-the-french-lines-ss-normandie-the-greatest-liner-ever-to-sail-across-the-pond-will-the-ss-united-states-and-qe-2-face-a-similar-demise/. Accessed 6 Sept. 2018.

Munger, S. *A Testament to Human Stupidity: The Sad Fate of the S.S. Normandie*. 9 Feb. 2015, seanmunger.com/2015/02/09/a-testament-to-human-stupidity-the-sad-fate-of-the-s-s-normandie/. Accessed 6 Sept. 2018.

Diehl, L B. *Smoke Over Manhattan: The Fate of the SS Normandie*. 29 Jan. 2010, www.historynet.com/the-fate-of-the-ss-normandie.htm. Accessed 6 Sept. 2018.

Klein, C. *What Was Operation Underworld?* 28 Oct. 2015, www.history.com/news/what-was-operation-underworld. Accessed 6 Sept. 2018.

Curtis, R D. *Thelma "Teddy" Scheer Lansky*. 7 June 2007, www.findagrave.com/memorial/19769458/thelma-lansky. Accessed 6 Sept. 2018.

Editors, F L. *Meyer Lansky's Step-Granddaughter Speaks ...* 2008, www.thefreelibrary.com/Meyer Lansky's step-granddaughter speaks ...-a0205033016. Accessed 6 Sept. 2018.

Editors, M A. *The Meyer Lansky Scrapbook*. 31 Dec. 2012, miamiarchives.blogspot.com/2012/12/the-meyer-lansky-scrapbook.html. Accessed 6 Sept. 2018.

Editors, C I. *Meyer Lansky, the Man behind "The Flamingo"*. 2017, www.casinoinside.ro/meyer-lansky-omul-din-spatele-lui-„flamingo/?lang=en. Accessed 6 Sept. 2018.

Editors, A M. *Meyer Lansky – Money Man to the Mob*. 15 June 2015, americanmafiahistory.com/meyer-lansky-money-man-to-the-mob/. Accessed 6 Sept. 2018.

Camacho, P. *Meyer Lansky: The Godfather of Money-Laundering*. 9 May 2017, www.linkedin.com/pulse/meyer-lansky-godfather-money-laundering-paul-camacho. Accessed 6 Sept. 2018.

Koch, E, and M Manning. *Mob Ties*. 15 May 2008, lasvegassun.com/news/2008/may/15/mob-ties/. Accessed 6 Sept. 2018.

Green, D B. *This Day in Jewish History 1983: A Crime Boss Cashes in His Chips*. 15 Jan. 2013, www.haaretz.com/jewish/.premium-1983-a-crime-boss-cashes-in-his-chips-1.5224582. Accessed 6 Sept. 2018.

Pryor, A. (2001). *Outlaws and Gunslingers*. Stagecoach Publishing.

The Mystery of Meyer Lansky [Television series episode]. (2012). In *Mafia's Greatest Hits*. The History Channel.

Free Books by Charles River Editors

We have brand new titles available for free most days of the week. To see which of our titles are currently free, click on this link.

Discounted Books by Charles River Editors

We have titles at a discount price of just 99 cents everyday. To see which of our titles are currently 99 cents, click on this link.

Printed in Great Britain
by Amazon

47754557R00030